MW01100535

NORTH DAKOTA
A PHOTOGRAPHIC CELEBRATION

AMERICAN & WORLD GEOGRAPHIC PUBLISHING

CHUCK HANEY

Above: *Prairie wildflowers grace Fort Ransom State Park in the Sheyenne River Valley.*
Right: *Looking over Fargo toward Moorhead, Minnesota.*
Title page: *Morning awakens.* CHARLIE BORLAND

Front cover: *Red River Valley.* G. ALAN NELSON

Back cover: *The Little Missouri River Valley from Oxbow Overlook, Theodore Roosevelt National Park.* CHARLIE BORLAND

ISBN 1-56037-020-3

© 1994 Unicorn Publishing, Inc.

Write for our catalog:
American & World Geographic Publishing, P.O. Box 5630, Helena, MT 59604.
Printed in U.S.A. by Fenske Companies, Billings, Montana.

Right: *Yellow-headed blackbird.*
Below: *Alfalfa-harvest pattern.*

Facing page: *Heading for the pot of gold in the Turtle Mountains.*

Following spread: *From Riverdale, snaking up the Missouri for 200 miles, it's Lake Sakakawea.* LARRY MAYER

GLENN VAN NIMWEGEN

LARRY MAYER

Above: *Walleye—comin' right at ya!*

Facing page: *Fingers of Lake Sakakawea reach out to touch the dawn.*

Above: *Leisurely travel in the Badlands.*
Facing page: *The Ringsakker schoolhouse near Cooperstown.*

CLAYTON WOLT

CRAIG BIHRLE

KEITH KRAMER

Above: *A summer afternoon, a pole in Crappie Creek, and all's right with his world.*
Left: *In January, the fishing derby action is at Devils Lake.*

Facing page: *The riverboat Lewis & Clark carries passengers from Bismarck to Fort Abraham Lincoln State Park in grand old style.*

13

Left: North Dakota's magnificent Art Deco capitol rises 19 stories above the state government complex in Bismarck.
Above: On the capitol grounds stands this memorial to the hopes of many North Dakota settlers.

Above: *In Mercer County.*
Facing page: *Little Missouri Bay State Park.*

CLAYTON WOLT

DAWN CHARGING

Above: *Is a Devils Lake farmer signalling aliens?*

Facing page, top: *Western prairie fringed orchid.*
Bottom: *Cold and abandoned.*

Overleaf: *A landscape pattern at Bismarck catches the pilot's eye.*

LARRY MAYER

Above: *Can this barn owl be lord of all he surveys?*
Left: *October sunset lights a Morton County barn.*

DAPHNE KINZLER

Above: *Snow geese fill the sky above the James River Valley.*
Facing page: *The town of White Earth in the White Earth River Valley.*

Following spread: *Little Missouri Bay on Lake Sakakawea.* LARRY MAYER

LARRY MAYER

25

The rich Red River Valley north of Fargo.

Left: Swathing barley in Steele County.
Below: A concrete cow at New Salem is an arresting sight even from the sky.

Left: University town and commercial hub on the Red River of the North—Grand Forks.
Above: Wild prairie roses—the state flower—abloom in Turtle River State Park.
Top: Floral clock at the International Peace Gardens on the Manitoba border.
Overleaf: The town of Devils Lake, named for its neighbor, the largest natural body of water in the state.

Left: *Gathered for a pow-wow at Cannon Ball on the Standing Rock Indian Reservation.*
Below: *Competitor in Men's Traditional dancing at United Tribes Pow-wow, Bismarck.*

Facing page: *Autumn gold along Burnt Boat Drive, Bismarck.*

Overleaf: *The Yellowstone River joins the Mighty Mo.*

MICHAEL EVANS/THE IMAGE FINDERS

Above: *Confluence of the Heart and Missouri rivers in Fort Abraham Lincoln State Park.*

Facing page: *Fort Union Trading Post National Historic Site near Williston places visitors in an accurate reproduction of the post founded in 1829 and active until 1867.*

Left: *Since 1989, the Bismarck/
Mandan Folkfest has been an annual
delight.*
Below: *Planning ahead—Oakes
Irrigation Days parade.*

Opening flag ceremony at Mandan Rodeo Days, a Fourth of July tradition for more than a century.

Above: *Successful pheasant hunter on Oahe Wildlife Management Area.*

Facing page: *A royal sunset east of Minot.*

SHELDON GREEN

Above: Downhill skiers flock to Huff Hills south of Mandan.
Left: After an ice storm near Luverne, mere cottonwoods become magical.

Above: *Now arriving Bismarck.*

Facing page, top: *Capturing a fellow flyer above the pattern of sewage lagoons, Devils Lake.*
Bottom: *Visitors to the airshow segment of the Bismarck Mandan Folkfest turn away from a shining DC-3 airliner to watch an aerobatic exhibition.*

LARRY MAYER

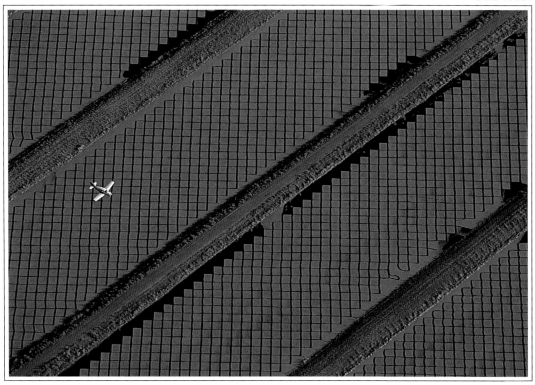

JEFF OLSON

47

Sunrise chases mist from the Little Missouri River

49

Above: A snake of a highway through Theodore Roosevelt National Park.
Facing page: In the park's south unit, Wind Canyon of the Little Missouri River.

Sentinal Butte rises 1,046 feet above the Badlands.

On the one-time Maltese Cross Ranch, which boasted Theodore Roosevelt as a partner.

CHARLIE BORLAND

Winter storm's end on the North Unit.

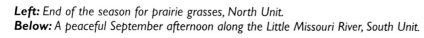

Left: *End of the season for prairie grasses, North Unit.*
Below: *A peaceful September afternoon along the Little Missouri River, South Unit.*

JEFF GNASS

Sculpture by Nature, in the South Unit.

57

Whitetail buck in the Park.

Along the South Unit's Scenic Loop Drive, badlands meet short-grass prairie.

Above: *Goldenweed abloom in the South Unit.*
Facing page, top: *The Park's free-ranging bison herd is one of its great attractions.* **Bottom:** *Wind Canyon cliffs.*

Just a dusting—in the North Unit.

RICHARD LONGSETH

Near the Squaw Creek Campground, North Unit, on an October day.

Denizens of the south Unit's Petrified Forest.

Left: *Coneflowers dot the Park's grasslands.*
Above: *View from the North Unit's River Bend Overlook down to the Little Missouri.*

Along Scenic Loop Drive, South Unit.

Badlands? Or, wonder-lands? Above Little Missouri, South Unit.

Aptly named cannonball
formations in the North Unit.

Below: *Sequoia stump, Petrified Forest.*
Facing page: *Eroded landscape near Peaceful Valley, South Unit.*

LARRY ULRICH

CHARLIE BORLAND

Above: *Killdeer Mountains ranch.*
Right: *Long-distance perspective in Billings County.*
Facing page, top: *Little Missouri National Grassland, McKenzie County.*
Following spread: *Aerial view of boaters enjoying Lake Metigoshe.* LARRY MAYER

Left: At sundown south of New Salem, prepared for the night's hunt.
Below: Wheat harvest time in Steele County.
Facing page: Beyond the blue horizon in the Red River Valley.

Left: *Welcome to the birthplace of the Champagne Musicmaker himself, Lawrence Welk of Strasburg.*
Below: *Reconstructed at Fort Abraham Lincoln, the home of George and Libbie Custer.*
Facing page: *Cottonwoods in winter garb.*

CHARLIE BORLAND

Above: Step back into the 19th century at Sunne Demonstration Farm in Fort Ransom State Park.

Facing page: Reconstructed blockhouse and stockade at Fort Abercrombie State Historic Site between Fargo and Wahpeton.

Overleaf: Gittin' along through the Badlands. CLAYTON WOLT

In Medora, memories of the colorful Marquis de Mores and of rancher Teddy Roosevelt live on.

Joining sister cities Bismarck and Mandan on the Missouri.

Above: *North Dakota State University, Fargo, fields the Bison before enthusiastic fans.*

Facing page bottom: *The Fighting Sioux take to the ice to defend the honor of University of North Dakota, Grand Forks.*
Top: *Future stars participate in the Youth Hockey League at Bismarck.*

CLAYTON WOLT

LARRY MAYER

Every June at Fort Abraham Lincoln State Park, the 7th Cavalry rides and shoots again.

Fort Union Trading Post, the largest on the upper Missouri, served the American Fur Company.

Left: *Bonanzaville, U.S.A., west of West Fargo, demonstrates life in the Bonanza Farm era.*
Below: *A Griggs County Lutheran church basks in the sun of high summer.*

Facing page: *Bird's-eye view of farm land near Devils Lake.* LARRY MAYER

Above: Benedictines founded Assumption Abbey at Richardton in 1899.
Facing page, top: Enjoying the Missouri downstream from Bismarck.
Bottom: At Minot's annual Norsk Høstfest, folk dancers entertain and also pass along Norwegian traditional style.

Autumn sunrise in Cass County.